THE WIND ON MY
GRANDMOTHER'S GRAVE

BRIAN FLATGARD LIVED an idyllic and pastoral childhood
in the small town of Windom, Minnesota. As an adult, he
moved to Phoenix, Arizona. In the mid-1990s, founded
Chiswell Street Press and published many Phoenix poets
As a slam poet, Flatgard participated in International
Poetry Slams. He currently lives in downtown Phoenix
with his daughter and is at work on a memoir about his
father. Learn more at WWW·BRIANFLATGARD·COM.

OTHER BOOKS BY BRIAN FLATGARD

Let Loose Passion: The Birth of a Poet

Bottles, Bigots & Beyond:
Poetry from the members of vox inc, written with
Dale Anderson, Leslie Barton, Jules Dinehdeal,
George Gilcrease, John Good, David LaSpaluto
and Pat Steward

Three Poets, One Car: Poems for a Road Trip,
written with David LaSpaluto and George Tirado

THE

W I N D

ON MY

Grandmother's Grave

To Carrie,
Hope you enjoy the poems!

[signature]

BRIAN FLATGARD

11/21/17 CHANGING HANDS PHX

The poem, "The Wind on My Grandmother's Grave,"
appeared in an earlier mini-book from Chiswell Street
Press, May 1993 and November 1993. "calm/the lake at
night/unseen," "raining/the ducks swim through the
sky," "Somehow," "While We Speed Through Monument
Valley" and "Conquistadors" appeared in different forms
in *Three Poets, One Car: Poems for a Road Trip,* August,
1993, Chiswell Street Press. "Daily Honey" and "Pole Star"
copyright © 2017 by Brian Flatgard.

Typeset in Caslon.

A limited first edition of forty books was published
December, 1993.

Second edition: March, 1994.

Third edition: November, 2017.
3.0

DEDICATION

TO THE MEMORY and spirit of my grandmothers, Malinda Flatgard and Alice Burton.

CONTENTS

1993 PREFACE

IN THE SUMMER OF 1993 I returned to my hometown, the small farming community of Windom, Minnesota. I left Windom about six years ago and usually return two or three times a year. I made the trip this time with my girlfriend, Leslie, from Phoenix, Arizona. We traveled for a vacation and to attend the family reunion of Malinda Flatgard's offspring, one of many reunions held by my relatives.

Since moving from Windom, my father, David, has taken up the paintbrush as a creative tool, and I have taken up the pen. Leslie is also a poet and painter, so we decided, half tongue-in-cheek, to give an art show and poetry reading. My sister, Stephanie, booked the local library for a weekend. We made up invitations and posters, and Steph and my other sister, Beth, hyped it around town as "A Brenda A. Flatgard Production" (my mother).

I'd been kicking around poems about Windom for a long time in my head, and I decided to let some out for the reading. I kept pen and paper ready in case one tried to escape, and one day, the image of my grandma Malinda's grave jumped to mind as Leslie and I biked to a coffeehouse. We got there, got a cup of coffee, and I brought my mind to her grave. And I felt the wind. The poem, *The Wind on My Grandmother's Grave*, flowed right out of the pen. One of the longest poems I've written, the pen wrote it pretty much as it is now, no rewrite, just a few words changed. I wept upon its completion: it was magical.

We spent the week hanging out, touring old haunts and meeting friends and relatives, many of whom had come to town for the reunion. We found ourselves host to a full house at the three readings we gave. The audience of friends and familiar faces was as responsive and loving as any we'd read to.

The depth of emotion after the reading of *The Wind on My Grandmother's Grave* was unforgettable. It was like taking the power of the poem when I first wrote it and intensifying that power by the number of people in the room. Reading the poem to a crowd of people who knew and loved Malinda has been one of the greatest blessings of my life. I am very thankful for the family I have.

And this has been the core of inspiration to create a whole book woven of my family and of Windom—a book of home.

Gilles Deleuze once said, "Always keep a piece of fresh land with you at all times." I agree with Deleuze, that it is important to keep a place in your heart you can return to no matter where you are. That's what I've tried to do with this book, create a place of home I can hold in my hands. I hope you find it warm and friendly.

Brian Flatgard
November 15, 1993

2017 PREFACE

SINCE THE FIRST PUBLICATION of this book over twenty years ago, a generational shift occurred. I wrote this poetry to commemorate the passing of my grandparents' generation. Today only a few great-uncles and great-aunts from that group remain. One still lives in the same farmhouse where he was born 93 years ago. A way of life goes with them.

It is now my parents' generation that dwindles. My sisters and cousins and I have entered that long middle age, caring for parents and children alike. I mourn my father and write of him. I look to my daughter and son and wonder how they will remember me.

Returning to poetry I wrote in my twenties is strange, joyous, and full of surprises. While I would write some poems and lines differently today, they continue to stand proudly on the page. Words I thought quite clever now feel flat. Some words I quickly read a hundred times—considering them mere stepping stones in the poem—now stop me cold and choke up my throat.

Republishing this book helps me see, yet again, the impermanence and ever-changing nature of life. It seems unthinkable that an entire generation can be swept away and only live in our memories, in stories we half-remembered as we walked by tombstones. Our understanding of the world is always changing, always wrong, always right. It is good to place markers to show where we were and then to move on.

Brian Flatgard
November, 2017

ACKNOWLEDGMENTS

I WISH TO thank my immediate family for their unconditional love over the years. Thanks to my folks, David and Brenda, I love you. And big love and thanks to my sisters, Beth and Stephanie, who have made me laugh far more than they could have picked on me. Your voices are in my writing.

ACKNOWLEDGMENT OF PATRONS

I CANNOT THANK enough the following people who supported this book as patrons. Without their help, it would have been impossible to create this book. To them I give my humblest thanks.

DAVID & BRENDA FLATGARD:
In memory of our parents, Oscar & Malinda Flatgard, Francis & Alice Burton.

STEPHANIE, JAMES, ERICA & DYLAN SMITH.

BETH, RAYMOND, NATHAN & ERIC LUND:
Commissioned with love for their children that they may cherish their family heritage and know the love that is their uncle.

M. CRISTINA GONZALES:
In memory of Spencer Bear Heels and Severt Young Bear.

KEN JANOVSKY:
For Maura Janovsky.

LYLE & STELLA PLATH:
In memory of Steven Dale Plath.

ORRIN & BETTY HOLMEN.

BRIAN BLOEDOW &. KAARI KORHONEN:
In memory of their friend, Daniel Cybyske, whose loyalty and inspiration will be greatly missed.

CHRISTINE M. DILAPI.

JANE SMITH.

JIM & JUNE BORSETH.

PATRICE & CHEYENNE MARIE FLATGARD:
Remembering special childhood memories of growing up on the farm in Bergen, Minnesota.

BRUCE WILLIAMS:
Bruce is Harder Than You.

WILLIAM H. ALBINSON:
In appreciation of a brilliantly sensitive and eloquent young talent who gives us many moments filled with humorous and provocative pleasure.

GEORGE VACEK.

KATHY & MARLYN VOEHL:
For our children, Mitchell and Michell.

NICK BACON:
For Diane K. Hughes.

JULES DINEHDEAL:
We are all Rain+Dancers.

ROBERT & SUSAN NAVARRO.

THE WIND ON MY GRANDMOTHER'S GRAVE

*Poetry from and for
a trip to Windom, Minnesota,
June 18 – June 28, 1993.*

A BOOK CALLED THE SOUL

There is a quality
of words on a written page,
the moſt banal attains importance,
juſt by the aᴄt of writing,
the smalleſt and dulleſt of moments
is given meaning.
Maybe that's why we enter our births in official records,
why we chisel the names of our dead in forever granite.

Is this an attempt to give our lives an importance
and permanence?

There is no need, reſt assured,
for are we not walking produᴄts of God's word?

Are we not,
each of us,
a word in God's great book?

Are we not,
each of us,
more than word, more than sentence or paragraph,
but in faᴄt
a grand and epic novel?
Each of us have ſtories that center to the core of our
    bodies as rings in a tree,
heroes in tragedy and in comedy,
breathing shouts and sighs and sleeps…

Don't we see the ſtories in each other's eyes
    a book

called
    the soul?

THE WIND ON MY
GRANDMOTHER'S GRAVE

I can feel the wind
on my grandmother's grave
wherever I am.

After gravel-road driving to the little Bergen church,
I fill the bucket that hangs from a spigot by the gate of
    the cemetery, water
for the flowers growing in the planters at the cluster of
    Flatgard graves.
How many times has this bucket been filled by me?
    by my family?
How many gallons of life
    have been hauled by the families of the Bergen dead?

Who plants these flowers and provides the dirt?
    my family? the church?
I'm not sure, but it's nice to think that every spring we
    pay our respect.
That every year we find it as much a part of life to sow
    the cemeteries as the farmers annual turning of the
    thick loam.
Are we growing hope?

    I can feel the wind
    on my grandmother's grave
    wherever I am.

Ah, this wind,
blowing from the green plains that roll for miles,
the fields nestle the church and cemetery,
whispering at the fence-line.
I remember at family gatherings,
me and my cousins, running
around this church, climbing
the trees of the graveyard, laughing

at city relatives who stood in the fields and said,
Take my picture in the corn
when we knew they were in the beans.

Was the wind blowing
    that day we put Grandma in the ground?
I believe I felt it.
I stood with five of my cousins,
we were men now, casket-bearers,
six abreast, strong in our suits,
facing the large crowd gathered at her open grave.
I felt rooted there with my cousins,
like a windbreak we got our strength from each other,
shoulder to shoulder,
looking at the familiar faces all sad,
friends and family,
from the wrinkled and old
    to the taut-skinned babies,
I saw my grandmother had not died,
no more than a stalk of corn that gives seeds before
    returning to earth,
to spring forth again as a multitude, my family,
we stand together and sway in the wind.

    I can feel the wind
    on my grandmother's grave
    wherever I am.

I remember thinking at my grandma's funeral,
we'll never gather this large again.
After the burial, we all went to my great-uncle's
for grandma's favorite way to celebrate,
    we gathered to eat.
We were jammed wall-to-wall,
    laughing and greeting
those we hadn't seen for so long,
hugs and back-slaps and farmer-strong handshakes.
Before the meal a hush,

we thought of Malinda
each of us in our own way and collectively,
then we sang our traditional table grace:

Be present at our table Lord,
Be here and everywhere adored,
These mercies bless and grant that we,
May feast in paradise with thee.
                    Ah-
                    men.

Oh,
who did not feel the power of that song,
all those voices becoming one voice.
We lifted Malinda to God on that voice.

We sang
    in sorrow for the one who was not with us.
We sang
    in joy to think of Grandma with her maker.
We sang Malinda,
    the song her love.
We sang Malinda
    and I saw her face smile before me again.

    I can feel the wind
    on my grandmother's grave
    wherever I am.

The air was still in the nursing home
where Grandma spent her last years.
She came in after a stroke,
thinking she was still in her own house, she'd say
Go in the kitchen and get more chairs now
as we crowded in her room to visit her.
But Malinda got better and better,
fought her own mind, cleared the fog.
Soon she'd ask to be taken back early when she visited us,
she had a card game to attend to.

She looked after the other residents,
and when I visited she showed me off,
reintroduced me to the people who forgot my name
     since our laſt introduction,
to the people paralyzed with ſtroke,
to the blind people who knew Grandma by voice,
to the people missing arms, missing legs, missing…

At beſt the people were like Malinda,
able to get around, sharp enough to visit,
but some were at their worſt,
lying on their back and juſt ſtaring,
     waiting,
          waiting,
               waiting…

I left the Home always thankful,
always renewed,
always inspired by these daily battles with death.
I left with a vow to live.

The air in the nursing home was ſtill,
a chemical smell, a food smell,
a smell between school and hospital,
always the same,
so it was with great joy
we got Grandma in the low bucket seat
of my Special Edition 6.6 Litre Trans-Am,
not sure how I was going to get her out again.
In the trunk was her walker and the removable sunroof.
We donned our sunglasses and blew outta town,
the nursing home blipped from the rearview mirror
     within seconds.

Roadtrip, juſt Grandma and me.
Our deſtination, Iowa.

Wind in her old lady hair,
we had small bits of conversation when slowing through
    farm towns
before kicking it down again,
    roar
of engine and wind,
that beautiful white noise of freedom.

We made this trip to see Grandma's sick friend,
it was the last time they'd see each other.
They talked in one room while I sat and tried to watch
    TV in the other,
instead thinking of what they could be saying to each
    other,
old friends burdened with the weight of parting.

It was extra important to live,
    live,
after that talk so Grandma and I cruised the resort lakes,
everybody else summer-cruising too,
seeing and being seen.
We saw it all and got the most looks,
for my car was much faster,
and my girl, much older.

Then to Godfather's for pizza and cokes,
food forbidden to Grandma at the nursing home,
we ordered not a small,
    not a medium,
        but a large of everything. That day,

the food was so good,
the iced pop so cold, fizz sparkling in our head,
the fields rolling by so green,
the lakes so blue
    with bright white-caps,
the sky so blue
    with white clouds,

all the people out living,
fat and skinny and old and young,
   outside,
      in water,
         on sand,
      on boats,
     on roller coasters,
the sun like a bright spotlight from God,
brightly illuminating this grand play he had staged.
This is how Grandma fell asleep on the car-ride home,
   at peace,
she slept contentedly with a full stomach,
the warm sun on her face.

Coming home, we passed the Bergen church,
yet I didn't think that Grandma would lay there one day,
for there she was next to me,
sleeping calmly and happily from such a full day,
a full day of sorrow and joy and sun and wind,
blowing
   blowing
      blowing
as we traveled together
the web of long roads that connect us all.

   I can feel the wind
   on my grandmother's grave
   wherever I am.

A FATHER'S ADVICE

My dad always said,
Pee in the middle of the toilet,
then they know you got something.

When I went to college he told me,
Don't drink vodka. People can't smell it
and they'll think you're stupid.

That's about all the advice he outright gave me.
For years he has let me screw up in silence,

and that quiet advice is just beginning to be clear to me.

DETAIL OF FATHER AND SON

"It's the little details that make it,"
my father and I agree,
as we talk art and poetry down the freeway.
Dad talks about his new watered-down blue-green
    painting technique,
something that will bring the painting off
yet nobody will notice
    the trick of it,
and as he talks he looks ahead at traffic and sky,
envisioning paint and water blending to his new color.

I sit in the passenger seat,
and dad, my old man,
I notice
    you like a hawk,
cuz I'm turning into you.

When I was young I was exasperated
when each year you had two and only two things
on your Christmas list:
    socks and underwear.
To my dismay, I unwittingly added underwear to my
    Christmas list this year,
in a few more years I'll enjoy receiving
    oh boy
socks.

I inherited your height
and when I bump my head I'm horrified,
not about finding blood,
but that I reflexively check for blood the
    exact
    same
    way
you do,
applying open palm to the forehead

and then examining my hand for red spots,
one of your many nuances
that are becoming mine.

I inherited your blood,
a secret mixture nobody notices,
bringing me to a height where I see
we got something good going down this freeway,
a simple father who paints,
and his simple son, who writes poems.

INGA

Old Aunt Inga
was a snoopy one,
mouthed to everybody what her nose found,
and one day on the way to church arrived early
to pick up my grandmother, running late.

Grandma hid the dirty dishes in the cupboards,
the cups here, the silverware there,
a big bowl of gravy on the highest shelf.

Grandma went upstairs to change into her church
     clothes
and when she came down, there Aunt Inga stood
below the open cupboard,
covered with gravy,
nose and all.

A POEM FOR MY MOTHER

My god,
how can I be so lucky?
My God,
I thank you.

To sit here with my mother on a Saturday night
who in all my 24 years
has not raised her voice to me,
never an unkind word,

has this ever happened in history?
That a mother and son share no hard feelings,
no slights,
at least none I've felt
and I'll admit
I'm innocent of the pain I cause others
but this is a miracle, yes,
that my mother and I sit here
sharing not pain but a love,
listening to a mutual favorite radio station
Saturday night playing both mellow Grateful Dead
and scorchin' Stevie Ray, God rest his soul,

our chairs next to the fireplace,
the night spins on while we read,
dying embers between us,
we have out-read fire itself,
quoting occasionally from the books
we picked up just this afternoon,
in one of the many libraries we have visited together.

She told me when she was a kid
she climbed her favorite tree to read,
her Shirley Temple hair and farm grove leaves
    blowing in the wind.
Now here she is,

reading with the youngest branch of her blood.
The love of books she has cultivated in me
a small part of something bigger,

my mother my friend,
my mother my mother,
I love you,
I thank you.

POLE STAR

My dad was always the storyteller, the joker, the loud one
while my mom and I and my sisters had to listen
to the same build-ups and laugh lines over and over.

While my dad talked in blunt periods,
    loud exclamation points,
my mom talked in parentheses, in ellipses,
little question marks, or sometimes not at all.

She'd stay silent on a subject, sometimes
for years, and at the right moment tell me
a truth that was undeniable. A whisper
of a comment cushioned in soft words,
a butterfly effect to nudge me in the right direction.

My mom wasn't all humility though. To this day,
she's quick on the accelerator.

When I was a kid, her mother lived in Rochester,
150 miles away, and we'd consistently get there
in less than 150 minutes.

When she and I took trips together,
we sometimes missed an exit or turn
as our focus was on a driving alphabet game,
finding each letter, in order,
on road signs or car licenses or tractor-trailer graphics.
My mom was fun.

Once, and this was in the days
when I and all good Americans
were enraptured with semi-trucks
    —*Smokey & the Bandit* and convoy songs—
we were in our '69 Cadillac convertible,
top down, barreling back home on Interstate 90,
and my mom used the I-NINETY sign

not only as her speed limit,
but as a command.
Each truck we passed picked up speed, and tailed us
on the correct logic that any state trooper
would pull over the lead top-down pedal-down Caddy
with the brilliant red hood as long as an aircraft carrier
    landing deck.
By the time we took the Jackson exit,
we were pulling two dozen semis in our wake,
and they saluted us with loud blasts of their horns
as we slowed and turned north
and they kept rolling west to the Dakotas.

I was in heaven.

At home, I excitedly told my dad, who grinned and said
Well, they were probably happy to follow your mom
and my parents laughed in this kinda different way.
I imagined the view from the high cab of those trucks
    and realized oh,
my mom's hot!

She also had, at various times,
a couple of Ford Mustangs,
a '65 zippy convertible,
and a tamer mid-70s Mustang with a moon roof,
both white.

I was really young then,
with a Curious George constellation book,
and we'd drive out into the country,
pull over on a side road, and sit
in one of those cars. Above us, through open roof,
in dark, rural, Minnesota, the sky was alive with stars to
    hunt.

Just the rustling of corn and soybeans and ditchweeds
and the turning of cartooned starbook pages.

If it was cool, she'd leave the heater on
and the Mustang's hum joined the night bugs' calls.

To sound like an old man,
when I was a kid, we watched the night sky for fun.
When there were meteor showers, my folks invited
other families for viewing parties at our house,
one side of our backyard had a fire going,
one side reserved for darkness,
with lawn chairs reclined all the way back
so you could watch the space dust sparkle the sky,
us kids in sleeping bags to stay warm, falling
asleep during the show, parents laughing and singing
by the fire, revelry and revelation.

But those back road sky watching trips were always quiet,
    drawn out, when it was just mom and me.

One night, there was to be a huge meteor
passing through, the biggest for decades.
We positioned the car, facing the expected path of entry,
    and waited. And waited.
And waited.

Like a lot of our grand expectations in life, it never came.

So we went home, not sad or disappointed,
good enough to just hang out, safe in the darkness.

I was out of the car first, at the entrance to our house,
and pivoting with the opening door, I faced my mom,
    who was walking towards me.
In that turning moment, in the sky,
a white rocket,
    a ghost,
an angel of destruction, roared
at us, emerging over
the neighbor's house, buzzing tree tops,

over my mom's head and in that long second
I thought it would slam into our house,
and whether I ducked or cried out or peed myself
I can't remember.

As it cleared our yard and whooshed
over our roof all I wanted to do was go inside to safety.

Of course it was that meteor,
which my mom never saw
except through my wide eyes.

That meteor affected me in an unearthly way
I'll never forget. My whole life
I had vivid memories of that loud and stunning event,
until well into adulthood when I realized
it couldn't have made any noise at all.
The speed of light and sound do not match.
That wide and white true line,
so vivid in my childhood,
was in fact silent.

And so it is with my mother, the soft-spoken one,
whose quiet words and gentle ways
form uncountable constellations which fill my worldview
    and there,
look up, there is the bright path
I cannot help but follow.

FAINT OF HEART

Old Aunt Inga opened the door
to see the young man who'd come calling
for her daughter.
The young man, excited and nervous,
had just donated blood to the Red Cross.

Aunt Inga peered through her bifocals,
    down
    her
    nose
at the faint and charitable man on the doorstep.

Inga saw the I-GAVE-BLOOD sticker on his chest,
now forgotten by the man,
and declared her approval in her boisterous Norwegian
    accent:
Oh, I see you've got a heart on!
and showed the flustered gentleman the way in to her
    daughter.

EIGHTEEN IS ENOUGH

My grandmother Alice was the last of eighteen children,
and according to legend,
her aging father named her in this way,
holding her at birth and announcing in German,
Das ist Alles.

SLOWLY, THE SHINE

My mother tells me stories of her father,
a woodworker when farming gave him time.
He built the writing desk given to me,
which waits in Minnesota until I get a home.

I grew up with that desk, but not its builder,
for my grandpa died when I was two.
The desk has lasted years,
always glowing in a corner of the house.
I think of him and the hours
he must've spent in his tin shed, creating.
Mom tells me he rubbed and rubbed
the linseed oil into his wood.
The desk still shines.

And I sit and write these poems,
working and working the words in my head
and I am trying, grandfather I never knew,
to make them shine.

WHEN GRANDMA LIVED
JUST THREE HOUSES AWAY

Remembering my grandmother Alice,
cigarette smoke and a story
rising from her ever-creaking Lazyboy.

She covers me in warm attention
like the heavy afghans she knits for my family.

The radio is silent,
she turned off the baseball game when I arrived,
and a pile of books lie next to her like a sleeping dog,
closed and quiet,
waiting for me to leave.

ART

I got a new grandfather when grandma Alice married
    Art at the age of 61.
Art never had any kids, always a bit overwhelmed when
    the whole clan came to visit.
He and grandma played thermostat wars,
Alice would come from the hot kitchen and turn
the thermostat down, a minute later, Art would roar
the furnace back up, cranking the dial to 80
and letting everybody know
the kids are freezing, Alice.

We knew that although he loved us,
he was a bit relieved when we left,
like the time we saw him
through the picture window, unwinding
the vacuum cleaner cord
before we could even get out of the driveway.

DAILY HONEY

At my great-grandparents' house, a colony of bees
once nested under the eaves.

Rather than declare the bees a pest,
my ancestors chose live and let live.
The hive was over the kitchen window,
the bees and humans could watch each other make food.

As the hive grew and merged
into the wall of the house, honey flowed
oh so slowly and made its way
through the window frame and down
the inside of the pane of glass over the sink.

Each day there was enough
to scoop and scrape for a sweet treat,
to add to toast or coffee or tea.

I wonder what that's like.

Where's that balance,
that letting-go flowing point
where a problem of ours becomes instead
its own reward?

NOBODY'S FOOL

for my first illustrator, Nathan

Presenting my first chapbook to my immediate family,
my nephew glances at just one poem,
and with the honesty of the young proclaims,
This is gibberish!

And I, the naked emperor, can only laugh.

WHERE I'M COMING FROM

My four great-uncles' names are
Avie *(uvvy),* Dully, Si *(sigh)* and Milo.
Another couple related to me are Gummy & Bumpy,
and somewhere is a relative named Nummy with a son,
    Stump.

And I didn't think this was anything
too out of the ordinary until out-of-towners
responded to these names with spitting giggles.

I did not realize the landscape of my youth was "bleak"
until a college friend from the Cities made the comment
as we drove home for Christmas break.

But then, my friend didn't have the opportunity
to know what great men my uncles are,
and not growing up here, couldn't know
the wealth of stories and heritage
that hid under the dirt-blown snow
that muddied this land for miles.

MY COUSIN'S HANDS

When we were kids
my cousin and I dreamed our futures
from forts we built in haystacks.

We agreed paradise waited for us in Montana.
We decided we would get a ranch together,
ride around on horses all day
and do the work we wanted to do.
At night we'd go to town to dance with our girlfriends,
and they'd stay girlfriends, you bet,
cuz no way we were going to get married.

And looking up past the straw
we'd see nothing but bright blue sky,
big sky, Montana sky.
The world seemed easy then,
all you had to do was travel to where your dreams were
    waiting.

Something happened as we grew older,
and Montana wasn't it.

We laugh about those dreams now,
and our talk is different when it's just him and me and a
    few beers.
We grew up and grew apart,
we don't have the little daily stuff in common anymore,
so there's more silence than words,
but we are comfortable with it,
our kinship is deeper.
We sip our beers, and again, gaze into that distance.

My cousin flexes his hands and curses them.
My hands hurt all the time.
I don't know bow long I can keep working there.

He works at the meat-packing plant,
hard work in cold air,
one of the few places in this small town to work.
He's married, has a house,
there's nowhere else to go.

My hands hurt all the time.
It's all he has to say.
Somebody built square houses where the haystacks were

               and Montana

is out of reach anyway.

A FUNNY THING, COURAGE

Do...
> *you...*

my uncle Si says to me,
struggling with his tongue,
not the delicate tip
but with the thick base
that sits inert in the back of his mouth.

Do...
> *you...*

he tries again,
strong hand on my shoulder,
how many years since his stroke
shut down his brain like a computer in midprogram,
what remained set busily to retrain the parts of his mind
> wiped out,

including his speech,
and his tongue still stubbornly sits,
as we all do, gathered at this family reunion on picnic
> benches,

all eyes on Si,
his finger in the air,
> hanging, waiting to make his point...

The linger falters, then waves in the air
as his searching face breaks into a sly Si smile,
and he uses his original hesitation like a master of timing,
do ...
> *you ...*

ever forget what you were going to say?

We roar in laughter
strong in the outburst

and I think
these are the things that enable us to endure,
this is the subtle bravery unnamed.

JOSEPH SYNDROME

Thanksgiving yum yum
a table of food and relatives
a table of brown—
    turkey, gravy, stuffing, bread
fall leaves, brown
remains of harvest on the field, brown
grass in the ditches, brown—
we've all traveled to be at this big brown table,
yumming and yucking it up.

My Uncle Sam, appropriately, talks politics
his son Joseph at his side,
fidgeting *I'm hot*
and being shushed
we eat this infinite pile of food
and still li'l Joseph complains *I'm hot*
and Uncle Sam keeps talking about that damn Reagan
and Joseph's mom keeps shushing
and we're bloating
til finally poor Joseph plum overheats
and makes himself a family legend
in one bold act of creation—

At the Thanksgiving table,
Joseph vomits.

An incredible puke!
Joseph's ripe stomach, a wee bucket,
spouts from his wide mouth,
a flying tube o' food back on his plate,
in reverse film slo-mo'ed for all to savor.

And the miracle of it,
he didn't spill a drop.
The glob centered on his plate,
liquid flowing to the sides but not over,

and before Joseph lay a plate of mushy, chunky food,
—all brown.

Brown,
 like fall, brown,
like Thanksgiving,
Joseph's plate is brown—and no different from the plates
 set before us.
Forks hang in the air as our eyes go from Joseph's plate
 to our own, remarkably similar, and
Joseph's mother, needing something to do, desperately
 searches for something to wipe up.

Finally, it is Uncle Sam
 who breaks the hold of the vomit
Well, we know how Joseph feels about Reagan,
 and laughing,
we pick up our shovels and bend to it again.

CAROLYN ARRIVES

written for Bill Albinson in memory of his mother

Saint Peter is amazed
as Carolyn strides through the gates of heaven
and tells him a joke
he's never heard, he,
gatekeeper to paradise,
thought he'd heard it all, but

Carolyn has no time for chatting,
as purposeful as her morning walks,
dressed in her finest with the legs of a 19-year-old,
the high chin of a baroness,
she enters the Great Cathedral,
counts off the columns
and settles in her pew,

her pew,

ol' J. S. Bach approves her claim, nodding
from behind the organ,
spinning his fugues for a smiling God.

HEY, THAT AIN'T JIM

Cruising my hometown
borrowing my brother-in-law's pickup,
confused waves from people who now know
only half of this familiar driving unit.

IT'S A LIVING

Two men kick back on the tailgate of an orange truck,
9 AM donuts and coffee
they watch white STOP AHEAD paint dry on the road...

working for the County sure beats working.

ALONE ON THE DECK

A gusty day,
writing poetry by the lake,
covered with cottonwood seeds
caught in my hair and baseball cap like snow,

fallen branches on my unread books.

TASTING THE WORLD

I like drinking coffee outside,
bugs and all.

ALONE ON THE DOCK

Thinking he's unobserved;
the young boy stands at the end of the dock,
balanced on one foot,
spinning
slowly

the other foot

arms rise
push the wind

stork

crane

he re-invents ancient tai-chi

Raining.

The ducks swim through the sky.

calm

the lake at night

unseen

Watching the river flow past my childhood backyard,
a muskrat!

Oh, I'd forgotten
about my old friends the muskrats.

RAGGED DISCIPLES

I visit my family,
and ride a roller coaster of sugar and salt,
of coffee and beer,
washed down with laughs and cheap gossip
and why not?

Didn't Jesus hang out with all us sinners?
Weren't we his favorites,
us petty sinners?

We were interesting and sincere,
we are simple and honest
    in our sins and lies.

A WAY WILL BE FOUND

A roadtrip to Minnesota,
I return to Windom, my place of birth,
for a reunion of family.

My girlfriend and I leave Phoenix at midnight,
drive through the coyote night
pulled by a sunrise in the Navajo nation,
driving through the long monolith shadows of this
    Monument Valley morning,

this enormous land

we catch the Colorado river at Moab, Utah,
follow its muddy flowings into Colorado state
where freeway and river travel together,
and when they part again we choose the river,
abandon the interstate for a route that begins as a two-
    lane paved road,
we wind up against gravity's current
down to one lane and gravel,
and this
this
was the magic of this road trip,
forced to 15 MPH,
forced to see,
unlike the interstates, those TV's of the roads,
fast images seen through a glass tube,
radio providing soundtrack and commercials,
landscape soundbites,
billboards of corporations,
that part of America I don't care for,
monolithic and centralized,
all efficiency and no magic.

When the freeway followed the Colorado
we traveled on high-tech Jetson's pillars,

straight line over the river and through giant blasted
    tunnels in the mountain,
push-button idiot box view with no way to rewind,
no way to pause,
but now

on this little road
by the big Colorado
we can stop and get out,
unwind,
wow at the view,
snap pictures and throw rocks in the river.

We drive slow with the windows down,
hands out feeling the wind,
the river talking peace and rage to us,
and here on the river the people wave,
the few people we see,
kids playing on the road,

a man working on his tractor smiles when he waves,
something passes between us in our simple nods and
    smiles,
something in his eyes is reflected in his wave.
I feel we shared a moment of contentedness,
    maybe serenity,
a shared feeling of the land,
of the beauty he knew so well, living out here the tough
    river-valley life,
I recognized him for that
and he
could see it all for the first time through our gawking
    eyes,

I think he saw us kiss,
    me and Leslie standing near a one-lane bridge,
right after we circled to see the view,
and if he could've shouted and if I could've heard

he'd say *Grand ain't it?*
and he would be talking about it all,
not just this river,
or the land it conquers and is contained by,
but life in all its forms,
life in form of river, of rocks and of plants,
life in form of freedom and constraint,
life in balance,
life in the kiss of a woman,

sweet

Mother earth,
our roads and railroads built stupidly next to your most
powerful weapon, water,
you must laugh at our self-importance,
you must laugh at the fat men in high towers
thinking they control the world.
How I admire your restraint when you could take' em
down so easily,
dominoes on the beach,
or are you biding your time,
waiting for the right ironic moment to mess up
foundations built on sand?

It's here,
on these small roads,
I see the nation we are supposed to be.
Are we Americans rugged individuals?
Or are we small bands working together?
I say we are both when we are at our best,
in these small communities,
we pull in and pay high prices for gas,
locals smart-assing each other at the plywood hamburger
stand next to the gas station,
we are at our best, individuals in small groups,
like the guys we saw working on the railroad tracks along
the river,

a jumble of yellow Cats and white company pickups,
hard-hatters and baseball caps eating their lunch,
a few gave me a peace sign in response to my wave and
    long hair,
and they meant it!

Ah Colorado,
Oh America, this
is the part of the nation I believe in,
this is what keeps my respect for the flag,
the surprising kindness we find
despite the drive-by shootings in the news.

Is all this fear justified?

I know if we broke down out here in nowhere America
    someone would spend half a day helping us out,
I've always been rewarded for my belief in the soul of
    folk with their help,
trust someone and you'll get it back ten-fold,
yet in my travels I'm warned to
watch out for the freaks and creeps,
    watch out for the hucksters and
why don't you carry a gun?

This I have learned and this we all know,
that it is the poor,
those who have the least to give who will give the most,
that those who have more than enough are the ones that
    take,
the bigger the motor home
    the less likely you'll be invited in,
but pull into the camp of two loggers
    living out of their tent
and you'll get all their beer
and the last of their kerosene will be used to ignite a
    chunk of old-growth redwood they "found" and have
    been saving just for an all-nighter like this,

this,
is the America I love,
these people who talk about the weather,
    these people I love,
they immediately go for what we have in common,
and isn't that what tolerance is all about,
isn't that a democracy, sharing what is common,
and respecting differences, in silence if need be,
talking about all this damn rain,
how two years ago it was drought and they said the lakes
    would take decades to fill up again
but now, by gum,
we're sandbagging against the flood and it just goes to
    show ya you can't believe everything
they
say.

A gas station somewhere near the Colorado-Nebraska
    border:
out of the blue I'm asked
How do you like your new Geo Prizm?
I turn to the old guy now next to me like a found friend,
Well, we rented it, but yeah it's got some spunk when you get
    it going and the mileage is good but coming through the
    mountains it was sluggish,
and he tells me of how he came this close to buying
    a Geo Prizm himself if they weren't so dog-ugly
    to begin with but now they don't look too bad and
    points out the '86 Skylark he just bought and I hear of
    every car he's owned,
like I really do remember when they brought out that
    new line in '62 before I was born and I forget what a
    rush I was in to get out of the car and pee,
cuz now that we know each other through our cars I
    explain what this trip is about, seeing my family,
    and I even admit I'm a poet,
and he nods and says
    hmmm,

and I hear a bit about his kids he's traveling to see and
    where they moved. and I catch a whiff of a divorce
    he's had, a sad scene from the vibes I get,
    this man is lonely,
and I nod and I say
    hmmm,
and when we finally part we can say in all sincerity
Have a good trip and hope your car runs well for you.

And we're really saying

Oh take care, frail fellow human,
may life's engine run smooth and clean,

and know, my new friend,
that there are people out there like you,
know there are strangers who care about you
    unconditionally,
that when you break down in a land of strangers
    someone will provide,
provide without thinking,
for the mere reason that kindness was shown to them at
    some time,
or for the meager reason that

it is right,

which isn't reason at all, but faith,

a deep,
unspoken,
illogical and wild
faith.

I say to you old man
driving to your children in Colorado
in your '86 Skylark with the goofy transmission,
I say a way will always be found.

THE SMELL OF FRESH MEMORIES

After a week-long visit to Minnesota,
driving home,
by the time we cross into Iowa
I'm scribbling poems of our trip onto a tablet on the
  steering wheel
eye to page to road to page,
can of Coke between my legs,
sunflower seeds in mouth,
windows down, smell of skunk, silage,
rock n roll on stereo,
sunglasses and baseball cap,
girlfriend at my side, also pen in hand,
we write, flooded with experiences,

and when she stops writing
she gazes out the window,
rolls in her fingers a gift from our poetry reading,

a carnation
  along her sun-lit thigh

CONQUISTADORS

We conquered this land with straight lines,
roads and railroads,
sectioned and fenced into square furrowed fields,

but the land still rolls,
still floods,

and I wonder what kind of vengeance is circling our way
for driving out the Natives, the buffalo,
the millions murdered.

WHILE WE SPEED THROUGH
MONUMENT VALLEY

a Navajo woman walks slowly behind her sheep,
aided by walking stick and dog,

a long, brilliant, Southwest pink skirt,
bright white shirt and hat,

I imagine her skin to be like the weathered rocks
a story,
there is something in her walk,

deliberate, unpaced

the way she walks
    shows things I don't understand,

I see the things I know about
    do not matter

I see I know nothing.

FRIEND IN THE NIGHT

Night drive in the midst of a 28-hour run,
everybody asleep except me

and the moon

rises
to ride shotgun

speeding over the trees at my side,
lifting itself to keep me awake
dropping near dawn
without needing to fill up on gas once.

SOMEHOW

It is all okay,
for somewhere in Minnesota,
fighting wind,
flies a butterfly all white,
and somehow,
through sunrises and sunsets,
    through winds and rains,
through tornadoes that twist silos
    and drive pieces of straw through trunks of trees,

somehow through all this
the fine dust on its wings remains intact
somehow it flies and lives.

With this my worries vanish as if chaff,
I am left with nothing but grains of substance,
small and delicate things exposed,
and protected by something as small as the sky.

平川